# THE BEACH

Peter Asmussen

# THE BEACH

TRANSLATED BY DAVID DUCHIN

OBERON BOOKS
LONDON

First published in this translation in 2005 by Oberon Books Ltd
521 Caledonian Road, London N7 9RH
Tel: 020 7607 3637 / Fax: 020 7607 3629
e-mail: oberonbooks@btconnect.com
www.oberonbooks.com

A catalogue record for this book is available from the British
Library.

ISBN: 1 84002 629 4

Cover design copyright © Oberon Books 2005

# Characters

BENEDIKTE
VERNER

SANNE
JAN

*A dash '–' in the text indicates a flow.*
*Lines are replied to without a pause.*

*The Beach* was short-listed for the Gate Theatre's Translation Award 2004 and received a rehearsed reading at the Gate on 27 July 2004. It was first performed at Theatre 503 on 9 August 2005 with the following cast:

BENEDIKTE, Beth Aynsley
VERNER, Piers Harrisson
SANNE, Kate Donmall
JAN, Sam O'Mahony-Adams

Director, Elly Green
Designer, Jennie Rawlings
Lighting Designer, Celia Perry
Composer, Thomas Spencer

**The Gate Translation Award**

The Gate is delighted to have launched *The Beach*, which was chosen as a finalist for the 2004 Gate Translation Award from over fifty entries from around the world. The discovery of hidden riches in international drama is at the heart of the Gate's work, and the biennial award celebrates the unique role which translators play in this endeavour. For more information on the Translation Award, go to www.gatetheatre.co.uk

# YEAR 1

## Scene One

*The stage is split in two: two hotel rooms. In each room a door and a bed, a window. It is day.*

*The room on the right has drawn curtains. There is a bottle of champagne in a cooler in the middle of the floor. BENEDIKTE lies in the bed.*

*White curtains billow lazily up and down in the room on the left. JAN lies on the bed. SANNE is dressing. She has her back to him.*

SANNE: Five.

JAN: Four.

*The door opens, VERNER sticks his head in.*

VERNER: Oh, sorry.

*He disappears, closing the door after him.*

JAN: Did you say something? –

SANNE: No.

JAN: I've got lots of pictures. Otherwise I can't remember anything we do. Isn't it strange, you see a picture that says nothing and suddenly you remember everything. Completely stupid details. What was said. Who sat next to whom. What we ate. You build up a lot of pictures in four years.

SANNE: Five.

JAN: Four.

SANNE: Five years.

JAN: Four. And the first year we were newly-weds.

7

SANNE: That's the whole reason we were here. And it's five years since then. I don't want to discuss this! I don't feel like figuring it out. It's possible it was five years ago. It's possible it was four years ago. You would think it was eighty years ago.

JAN: I know exactly how long it's been.

*Door opens. VERNER sticks his head inside.*

VERNER: Sorry.

*He disappears again, closing the door after himself.*

JAN: I know exactly how long it's been. The first year we were newly-weds. Then came the second, when we took a chance and there was room.

SANNE: We were the only ones at the hotel.

JAN: You really do remember. And the third, what happened the third year? I can't remember. It's gone. No. I can't remember it. If only I had some pictures. And now – year four. The fourth year we're here.

SANNE: Well that proves it.

JAN: The third time was last year. What happened last year? –

SANNE: Last year? –

JAN: You know what the worst thing is? I forgot my camera. Next year we'll have no idea what we did.

SANNE: I wouldn't anyway.

*The door opens, VERNER sticks his head in.*

VERNER: Ah, sorry. This is too much.

*He disappears again, closing the door after himself.*

JAN: Who is that man? –

SANNE: What man? –

JAN: The man that came in. I've never seen him before.

SANNE: I heard someone last night.

JAN: Then he must have woken the hotel manager. Now I remember! Now I know what it was! –

SANNE: You have bad breath.

*JAN holds his hand in front of his face and tries to smell his breath.*

JAN: I can't smell anything.

SANNE: I noticed it when you kissed me.

JAN: Why didn't you say anything? Why didn't you say anything? –

SANNE: What was it, then? –

JAN: What? –

SANNE: The thing you could remember about last year.

JAN: I jumped into the water from that little boat we rented. I jumped right into a jellyfish.

SANNE: I rubbed cold cream into your back.

JAN: I was only burned on my face. There was only one jellyfish, and I landed on it. It was stuck to my face and we burned our fingers trying to get the legs off. I have a picture of myself with a red face. Don't you remember? I asked you to take a picture so we'd be able to keep it. Don't you remember when I asked you to take a picture of me?

SANNE: It was the high point of our holiday.

JAN: You weren't all that sober. We'd been drinking in the boat. In fact, we were pissed.

SANNE: I'm calmer that way.

*The door opens and VERNER comes in.*

VERNER: Oh, I'm so sorry. You must think I'm wasted. All the hallways here look the same, and all the doors in the hallways look the same. I keep getting lost.

JAN: What's your room number?

VERNER: Two hundred and twenty.

JAN: That's upstairs. This is number hundred and nineteen.

VERNER: Well that explains it.

JAN: The numbers are on the bottom of the door. All the way down by the floor.

VERNER: Sorry if I disturbed you.

*He disappears again, closing the door behind him.*

SANNE: I'm going downstairs. I always get hungry after.

JAN: I should have brought my pictures. Then we'd have something to talk about.

*She leaves the room. JAN stays on the bed. Silence.*

*In the room on the right BENEDIKTE sits up in bed.*

BENEDIKTE: Is that you? Verner is that you? –

*Silence. She lies down again. The door opens, VERNER sticks his head in and quickly closes the door. BENEDIKTE sits up in bed again.*

Is someone there? –

*She looks around, confused. Then she gets up and goes to the window. Looks out. Then she lies down again. VERNER enters.*

VERNER: Finally.

BENEDIKTE: Where have you been? –

VERNER: I couldn't find our room. They all look alike. You haven't been out while I was gone, have you? Imagine if we both went in to the wrong rooms.

BENEDIKTE: I haven't gone out.

VERNER: It's cosier in the daylight. And the beach looks good. Wide, with sand and rocks and dunes. It's shallow for a long way, a wading beach. Wait a second.

*He gets a camera.*

I want you in bed.

*He takes a picture of her.*

The sun is shining outside. There's almost no wind. It's just the right kind of day for lying on the beach doing nothing.

BENEDIKTE: I've missed you.

VERNER: Missed me? I've been gone for ten minutes. There wasn't a soul out there. I couldn't even find a slice of bread.

BENEDIKTE: I've missed you.

VERNER: We were supposed to be drinking champagne. You want to drink it now? –

BENEDIKTE: I don't want anything to drink. I don't want to drink.

VERNER: Maybe it's a trap? You think it's a gift from the hotel and you drink it and then it's added to the bill when you check out.

BENEDIKTE: I've got nothing against you drinking it.

VERNER: I think the manager runs this hotel alone. I haven't seen anyone else. He looks old. I can't figure out how he manages. But it's nice and clean here, isn't it?

BENEDIKTE: Will you hold me?

*VERNER holds her.*

I don't know if I like it here.

VERNER: We just got here.

BENEDIKTE: I don't like it.

VERNER: Well let's not be too hasty.

*He holds her more tightly.*

BENEDIKTE: I'm freezing.

VERNER: You need to eat something.

BENEDIKTE: I'm nauseous.

VERNER: You know what we should have taken with us? A radio. We should have taken a radio. Maybe there's somewhere nearby where we can buy one. Everything is easier with music. I didn't even manage to find a slice of bread. I'm still hungry. Really hungry. I'm going down to find something to eat. Don't we get breakfast? Wasn't there something about breakfast included? –

*He stands up, takes his camera.*

You coming? –

*Black.*

## Scene Two

*The hotel restaurant. Day. Many empty tables and chairs. The only person there is SANNE, eating her breakfast alone.*

*VERNER enters. He has his camera with him. He nods to SANNE and sits down.*

SANNE: You have to go up and get the food yourself.

VERNER: Oh. Thanks.

*VERNER stands and walks over to the buffet. SANNE remains seated. VERNER comes back with a plate of breakfast. He gives a friendly nod to SANNE.*

SANNE: May I take your sugar? –

VERNER: Of course.

*They both stand at the same time and walk toward each other. They stop, reach toward each other, slightly comic, and VERNER gives her the sugar. She smiles slightly. They sit again. Silence.*

Do you live here? –

SANNE: You arrived last night? –

VERNER: That was me.

SANNE: I heard you.

VERNER: What else should I ask you? –

SANNE: Have you been here before? –

VERNER: This is my first time. And you? –

SANNE: This is the fourth year.

VERNER: You must like it.

SANNE: We won't be coming back next year.

VERNER: Is this a bad place? –

SANNE: It's more about the clientele.

VERNER: It's my first time here.

*They keep eating.*

SANNE: You were the one that got lost this morning.

VERNER: Was that your room? The two of you? –

*JAN enters.*

JAN: I remembered one more thing.

*JAN sees VERNER, sits next to SANNE, lowers his voice.*

I remembered something else. It was last year I found that big piece of amber. You remember now? I gave it to you so you could have it made into some jewellery.

13

Remember? Remember it was last year? – That's the idiot that got lost this morning.

*JAN gives a friendly nod to VERNER, who does the same.*

VERNER: Sorry I disturbed you this morning.

JAN: No problem.

VERNER: All the rooms look alike. I didn't know the numbers were at the bottom of the doors. They're usually at eye-level.

SANNE: What's your name? –

VERNER: Verner. What's yours? –

SANNE: Sanne.

JAN: Jan.

VERNER: And you've been coming here for four years? –

JAN: Five. No, four. That's right. The last four years.

SANNE: Would you like to join us? –

VERNER: Thanks.

*VERNER stands, takes his plate and camera, walks to their table, and sits down.*

JAN: Is that your camera? –

VERNER: Are you into taking pictures, too? –

JAN: Usually. But I forgot mine this year.

VERNER: Borrow mine!

*He hands him the camera.*

JAN: A camera is a very personal thing.

*VERNER puts the camera away.*

VERNER: What is there to do here? –

SANNE: Nothing.

JAN: That's not true. First of all there's the beach. I gather
amber down on the beach. Last year I found such
a big piece I was forced to give it to my wife. And I
dive. I love diving. Then there's the vineyard. And the
museum. The museum is a little bit inland. Strangely
enough, we've never been there. I have no idea what
they've got there. I think it's a nature museum. They
don't have any standard tourist stuff. No restaurants or
discos or bars. Not even a pub.

VERNER: Is there anywhere I can buy a radio? –

JAN: A radio? The shop might be able to order one.
There's a shop a little way up the beach, by the car-
park. Do you need a radio? –

VERNER: Everything is easier with music.

SANNE: What for example? –

JAN: A radio! –

SANNE: I'm going to tell you just what a crap place you've
ended up in. There's fuck all to do. There's no music
and no place to go. If you want to have fun, you'll have
to make it yourself. There's a beach where you can find
amber that you can keep and take home. Our house is
full of amber. Teeny tiny pieces of amber everywhere.
You rarely find a piece big enough to do anything with.
Last time I found a big piece, but I haven't taken it
to a jeweller yet. The manager runs this place alone,
and his food and his service are nothing to write home
about. The only thing that's good about this place is
the absence of naked children. Children would die of
boredom here.

Whenever, against all odds, some people turn up to
stay, they're always strange, and want to be alone. More
coffee?

*BENEDIKTE enters.*

Just look at her. You wouldn't think she was on holiday, would you? –

JAN: Well we've been here four years in a row.

SANNE: Five actually.

JAN: Year after year. So it couldn't be all that bad.

*BENEDIKTE seats herself at another table.*

VERNER: Just a second.

*He stands and walks to BENEDIKTE, bends over to speak with her.*

JAN: I'm going for a walk on the beach, where I may find some more amber. If I do find another piece we could have a pair of earrings made for you.

*VERNER and BENEDIKTE cross to JAN and SANNE's table.*

VERNER: This is Benedikte. And this is Jan. And Sanne.

*They all nod to each other.*

Please sit down. May we join you? –

*JAN moves a chair over to BENEDIKTE, who sits.*

I'll bring you something.

*He exits in order to bring her something.*

JAN: Your husband couldn't find your room this morning. The room number is on the bottom of the door. That's quite unusual. You have to know where it is. Are you on holiday? Stupid question. What else would you be doing here?

*VERNER returns with breakfast for BENEDIKTE.*

VERNER: I'm looking forward to getting out on the beach. Should I just walk over, or are there some parts that are better than the others? –

JAN: If you just want to sun yourself and get in the water then the best place to go is right down there. The beach is long and there are some dips that are a little more private. Do you swim? –

VERNER: We love swimming.

JAN: Do you dive? –

BENEDIKTE: I must tell you: I'm so happy. I'm pregnant. It was my last chance. We tried for years with no luck. I can't imagine a life without children. Life isn't complete without children. Even so, if I hadn't gotten pregnant, I would have accepted it. I wouldn't have tried IVF. I would say to myself that fate has decided that I shouldn't have children. But I don't know what I would have done. Life would have lost its meaning for me. Everything would go black. I'm just so happy. Thankful.

VERNER: In short, we're happy. Do you have children? –

JAN: No.

SANNE: It's because we only fuck on holiday. That limits our chances.

JAN: The only problem is that it's very shallow. You're cold before you ever get in the water. You have to go a hundred metres out before it's deep enough.

VERNER: Is there a current? –

JAN: Not much.

VERNER: This morning while I was lost I came down here to find something to eat. I was starving. But I couldn't find anything. The manager hadn't put anything out yet. The only thing I found was the ocean in daylight. It was dark when we got here and we couldn't see anything. The water looks so blue and clean and inviting. I'm itching to hop in.

*Black.*

# Scene Three

*The two hotel rooms. Day. The room on the left is empty. BENEDIKTE and VERNER are in the room to the right. He is in his swimming trunks, drying himself. The champagne is still in its cooler. There's a knock at the door.*

VERNER: Come in.

*JAN enters.*

JAN: So this is how you live.

VERNER: This is how we live.

JAN: Champagne? –

VERNER: From the manager.

JAN: Perhaps congratulations are in order? –

VERNER: If you want.

JAN: The first time we came here it was our honeymoon.

VERNER: Congratulations.

JAN: How was the water? –

VERNER: Cold. Cold but good.

JAN: So what I said was right? –

VERNER: What did you say? –

JAN: That you get cold before you even get in.

VERNER: The water was cold.

JAN: Didn't you get cold on the way out? –

VERNER: I ran.

JAN: Did you go diving? –

VERNER: I never dive.

JAN: We ought to drink that champagne in your honour. –

BENEDIKTE: I don't want anything to drink. I don't want anything to drink.

JAN: Where did you come from? Have you been here the whole time? I hope I didn't say anything I shouldn't have. (*Laughs.*) Did I? I didn't say anything I shouldn't have, did I? I actually came by to say that if there was anything you wanted to see – the museum or the vineyard or whatever – then I would love to show it to you. When you go someplace new you never know where to go. So you just say the word and I'm ready. Just say the word. It was nice to see how you live.

*JAN exits. VERNER resumes drying himself.*

*Black.*

\* \* \*

*The two hotel rooms. Night. The door to the room on the left opens and the light is turned on. SANNE and JAN enter. They are drunk.*

SANNE: I want to fuck! – Fuck me! –

JAN: She's strange.

SANNE: Who? –

JAN: Benedikte. Isn't that her name, Benedikte? –

*SANNE pushes him away.*

SANNE: I don't know what her name is! –

*She throws herself on the bed.*

JAN: She's raving mad. You know what she said to me? While we were eating. The two of you were outside and

I didn't know what I should say to her. I sat there trying to think of what to say, but nothing came out.

Then all of a sudden she just spits it out. 'I would never lie on a beach. I don't understand how people can do that. If you sift a little bit in the sand with your fingers you can see that it's teeming with small animals. You'd be killing them all if you flopped down on the beach.' That's what she said. So I tried to get down to the core of what she was saying and said that the sand would distribute the weight so that it was nearly impossible to crush even the larger creatures living there. 'Evil creatures?' she said. 'No, larger ones,' I said, ' – lizards or crabs. That size.' Evil creatures. She's the evil creature. Are you asleep? –

*Silence. SANNE is in a deep sleep. In the room on the right VERNER enters and turns on the light. The champagne is still there. VERNER dances alone.*

He's a clown. And he's a bit much for a clown. A little too proud of his big stupid camera. Congratulations. Congratulations. What did you say? Yeah, what did you think I said you clown. Shit for brains. The hell with your 'oh it looks so blue and inviting'. How else should it look? You little creepy fucker.

*He crosses to SANNE, stands for a moment looking at her. Then he straddles her midriff. Strokes her face. She doesn't move, doesn't react. He bends down and kisses her. He stands, opens the door, turns out the light and exits.*

*There is a knock on the door in the room to the right. At first VERNER doesn't react. There's another knock, this time louder.*

VERNER: Yes? –

*JAN enters.*

JAN: Where did you go? –

VERNER: We went for a walk.

JAN: Where's Benedikte? –

VERNER: Out for a walk.

JAN: I didn't even see you leave. Isn't it a shame to let that champagne just sit there? Isn't it a shame? – Shouldn't we drink it to celebrate meeting each other? –

VERNER: Why don't you just take it? We won't drink it.

JAN: You know what? I think I just might. I think I just might open it. Do we have glasses? – We don't have glasses. What the hell, we'll drink it out of the bottle. We won't catch anything. What would we catch? We don't have anything we can catch.

*He takes the bottle and starts opening it. BENEDIKTE enters.*

BENEDIKTE: You can hold your hand up in front of your face and there's no hand. There are no stars. No sky. No light whatsoever. No sound. No voices. Nothing. I move my hand and I can hear the tiny bones inside.

JAN: It's stuck. I'll wiggle it.

BENEDIKTE: But I can't see it. I move forward. Carefully. Step by step. Feeling my way so I don't fall. I can hear my feet in the grass. I can hear twigs break under my weight. But I can't see where I'm going. I can only hear it.

VERNER: Would you like to go to sleep? –

*The cork flies out of the bottle with a bang.*

JAN: It worked! –

VERNER: Would you like to go to sleep? –

JAN: Nobody's going to sleep! We're going to drink! –

*He drinks from the bottle.*

And it tastes good, too! –

BENEDIKTE: I'm frightened.

VERNER: Of what? –

BENEDIKTE: I don't know.

VERNER: You have to be afraid of something. Is it the baby? –

BENEDIKTE: No, of course not.

JAN: Anybody want some? Anybody want some? –

VERNER: Then what is it? –

BENEDIKTE: I don't know.

VERNER: You're just frightened? –

BENEDIKTE: I'm just frightened. I'm just frightened.

JAN: Come on you two. Come on. Here! Have some! –

VERNER: I think it would be better if you go.

JAN: But the champagne –

VERNER: I think it's better.

JAN: Okay, okay. Can I take the bottle with me? –

VERNER: Take it.

*JAN exits. VERNER turns toward BENEDIKTE. JAN enters again.*

JAN: (*To VERNER.*) I need to ask you a favour. Will you take a picture of me and Sanne together? Will you? –

*He exits.*

VERNER: Let's go to bed.

*Black.*

# Scene 4

*The beach. SANNE is lying on her back sunbathing. A radio plays by her side. She sits up and waves out toward the water, beyond the audience. She lies down again.*

*VERNER enters.*

VERNER: Can he see us? –

SANNE: He's diving.

*VERNER sits.*

Where is Benedikte? –

VERNER: Up in the room. I think. I don't know. In the room. She was out walking. She said she wanted to lie down.

*Silence.*

Now he's waving.

SANNE: Then wave back.

VERNER: He sees me.

SANNE: He doesn't give a damn.

*VERNER waves.*

VERNER: Doesn't he? –

SANNE: Not a damn.

*Silence.*

VERNER: Isn't it nice with the radio? – Everything is easier with music.

*VERNER caresses her shoulder. SANNE doesn't move. He removes his hand. He smoothes over the spot on her shoulder where he touched her.*

SANNE: Is something crawling on me? –

VERNER: No.

SANNE: I can't stand bugs.

VERNER: There's nothing there.

*Silence.*

He's waving again.

SANNE: Then I ought to wave back.

*They both wave to JAN out in the water.*

VERNER: Why does he dive? –

SANNE: Why? Why does anyone dive? He likes being underwater. He feels lighter. He likes the silence. And the colours. He says colours are different underwater.

*She lies down again.*

He does a lot of strange stuff. Last year he found a clump of amber. The plan was that he'd have it made into jewellery. He talked about it all winter. First it was supposed to be a necklace. Then a brooch. Then he wanted to wait until he found another piece so he could make earrings. I hate amber jewellery. I hate amber. We have a window-sill at home covered with amber. Tiny, stupid little pieces of amber. I'm not a Neanderthal.

*Silence.*

VERNER: I took a picture of you the other day.

SANNE: Of who? –

VERNER: The two of you. You and him.

SANNE: I didn't notice.

VERNER: You were both asleep.

SANNE: Was it a good picture? –

VERNER: I don't know yet.

*VERNER waves out over the water. BENEDIKTE enters.*

Benedikte's coming.

*SANNE sits up. BENEDIKTE walks over to them.*

SANNE: Hi Benedikte.

VERNER: Have a seat. –

*BENEDIKTE sits.*

Jan is out diving.

SANNE: Don't you want to try the water? It's just out there and looks blue and clean.

VERNER: Jan's waving.

*VERNER and SANNE wave.*

Don't you want to wave, too? –

*Slowly, mechanically, BENEDIKTE waves toward the water.*

*Black.*

# YEAR 2

## Scene Five

*The two hotel rooms. Evening. The only light in the room to the left comes from a little lamp. SANNE is lying in bed. In the room to the right BENEDIKTE is sitting in bed. There are a few suitcases on the floor in front of her. After a while SANNE pulls the duvet up over her head. A hand emerges from the duvet and turns out the light. VERNER enters the room to the right.*

VERNER: The manager is drunk. He's drinking. What else is there to do here when the summer ends? There isn't a soul here. The only thing to do is get drunk. He was almost unintelligible. He was depressed. He says he can't cope with running the hotel any more. He's ashamed to take money for it. He offered to reduce the price for us, but I told him it was alright. Do you think that's alright? It's hardly expensive. He probably makes enough in these two months to cover the whole year. I'm going to go see if they're here this year.

*He exits. BENEDIKTE remains where she is. There is a sound of knocking on the door in the room to the left, but no one answers. A moment later, VERNER returns to BENEDIKTE.*

Shall we unpack? –

*VERNER starts unpacking. There's a knock on the door.*

Yes? –

*JAN enters.*

JAN: You're here!? –

*They shake hands.*

The manager's been drunk since we got here.

VERNER: There's not much else to do here in the winter.

JAN: I'm happy the two of you came. I wasn't sure you would.

VERNER: We never doubted we would.

JAN: It was nice being here with you last year. At least that's what I thought.

VERNER: Same here.

JAN: I've been looking forward to seeing you.

VERNER: Same here.

JAN: I hoped you would. I've been down to the beach. Are you going diving?

VERNER: In a few days. I've got a cold. Of course I've got a cold. It's the first day of my holiday. When else do you get a cold? –

JAN: There was an oil spill. A tanker ran aground. But they've cleaned most of it up. You almost can't see it. I haven't been diving yet. Maybe everything down there is covered with thick, black oil. Maybe we should try the museum this year. We should. We should know more about this place. Do you feel like going to the museum? Do you? –

VERNER: I remembered to bring the radio. We had such a hard time getting it. I'm surprised we didn't forget it. I remember how nice it was with a little music. Everything is easier with music.

JAN: And you know what I remembered? My camera. I feel naked without my camera. I can't keep track of what I do without pictures.

VERNER: I've got something with me.

*VERNER takes out a photo and gives it to JAN.*

JAN: It's of us. We're asleep. We're in the hotel room and sleeping. I don't remember this one.

VERNER: You were sleeping.

JAN: We must have been drunk.

VERNER: You were.

JAN: How did you take it? –

VERNER: I couldn't sleep and decided to get up. I don't remember what we'd been doing. I think Benedikte was sleeping. She was. She fell asleep and I couldn't sleep. I came over to see if you were up. You'd forgot to lock the door. At first I couldn't see anything. Then I saw the two of you. It's just like in the picture. I went back and got my camera and took the picture.

JAN: Isn't that a bottle of champagne next to me? –

VERNER: That's Sanne.

JAN: It's all starting to come back. I remember something about the bottle – I couldn't get it open. Is that right? I couldn't get it open? –

VERNER: I can't remember.

JAN: I remember I couldn't get it open. But that's where my memory stops. Now I remember. That was the bottle you got from the manager, wasn't it? That was the bottle you got from the manager. Strange to see yourself in a picture you didn't know was taken. Now I remember! I'm so stupid. I was waiting for you. Where's the baby? Where's the baby? –

*VERNER tries to quiet JAN. BENEDIKTE sits frozen. Then she laughs. Happy and violent.*

*Black.*

* * *

*The two hotel rooms. Day. In the room to the left someone is sleeping, covered with a duvet. The curtains are drawn. The person in the bed can't be seen. In the room to the right stands BENEDIKTE, fully clothed. VERNER is putting his clothes on.*

VERNER: Can I come? –

BENEDIKTE: No.

*She leaves the room. VERNER finishes dressing and then exits. A moment later there's a soft knock at the door in the room to the left. No answer. Another soft knock. Then the door opens and VERNER enters. He walks to the bed.*

VERNER: Sanne? Sanne? –

*He begins to carefully caress the sleeping figure. Suddenly the figure wakes and sits up.*

JAN: What time is it? –

VERNER: I was on my way to the beach.

JAN: Dressed like that? –

VERNER: I'm going to change. Want to come? –

JAN: I haven't eaten.

*JAN gets up and opens the curtains.*

Now it's my turn to take a picture.

*He raises his camera, takes a picture of VERNER.*

I'm sorry for asking about the baby. That was stupid of me. What have you been up to this year? What have you been doing? –

VERNER: The job.

JAN: The job? What do you actually do? –

VERNER: I work for the civil service.

JAN: That's strange. I usually hate people that have jobs. But you I like.

VERNER: What do you do? –

JAN: Don't you know? –

VERNER: If I asked you before, I've forgotten.

JAN: I've got my own thing. I'm one of the people that keeps the wheels turning so you can get your pay. I'm only joking. I really do like you. What else have you been up to? –

VERNER: Taking care of Benedikte.

JAN: Is she very sad? –

VERNER: What do you think? –

JAN: Are you? –

VERNER: It's none of your business.

JAN: How did it happen? –

VERNER: How do things like this happen? –

JAN: It's terrible.

VERNER: We'll get over it.

JAN: You can always get over it.

VERNER: Have you tried? –

JAN: We haven't even got close.

VERNER: Do you want to? –

JAN: It's none of your business. There! – now I've got a lot of pictures of you.

*Black.*

# Scene Six

*The beach. SANNE is sunbathing. VERNER enters. He's carrying the radio. He sits a little way from SANNE. SANNE doesn't move. He turns on the radio. SANNE is motionless. VERNER turns off the radio.*

VERNER: Want to hear something strange? Do you? Do you want to hear something strange? – All those little pieces of amber. I can't forget all the little pieces of amber on the window-sill. Why do you think I would remember something like that? Those stupid bits of amber on the window-sill. I can't forget them. I've never seen anything so inane. Last winter I thought about the beach a lot. I longed to come back to it. I would think: if only there was something I could do. Snap my fingers, and then appear on the beach. I went in to see you this morning. Or at least I thought I did. But it wasn't you. There are so many things I wanted to know about you that I never found out. I pictured you standing in the garden. Do you ever do that? Do you ever stand out in the garden? In your garden, do you?

*SANNE raises herself up.*

SANNE: Was Jan sleeping? –

VERNER: I woke him up.

SANNE: Why did you stop calling? –

VERNER: We never thought we'd come back. But everything else was sold out. So we tried this place as our last resort. It was actually her idea. And of course, there was room here.

SANNE: Was that why? –

VERNER: Why what? –

SANNE: The baby. Or no baby.

VERNER: Naw.

SANNE: Why then? –

VERNER: I don't know what you mean. –

SANNE: Why did you stop calling? –

VERNER: It's the baby. Or, it was the baby. It was a bit much to be placed on such small, unborn shoulders. Benedikte. I couldn't do that to her. Do you know what the strangest thing is about your house? – The window-sill with the amber on it. What have you been doing? –

SANNE: Trying to get a little sun on my body.

VERNER: Every day? –

SANNE: Trying to get a little sun on my body. Does that matter any more?

VERNER: Not for me.

SANNE: I have a little shop that sells small sweet things for small sweet homes.

VERNER: Would you like to know what I do? –

SANNE: No.

*She lies down again.*

VERNER: You could have called. If you wanted to, you could have called.

*Silence.*

Want to know something strange? All of a sudden I'm scared of her.

SANNE: Who? –

VERNER: Benedikte. I've become scared of her.

*SANNE laughs.*

I ended up looking at her body this winter. Looking at it. Really looking at it. When we make love I usually skirt alongside it with my eyes. Avoid it. As close as possible so I can't see. But I saw it. I saw it from a distance. I didn't avoid it. I can see the difference from when we first met. I remember it as it was. It's gotten old.

*SANNE sits up.*

SANNE: Shhh! –

VERNER: Sorry.

SANNE: Shhh!

VERNER: What? –

SANNE: Someone's singing.

VERNER: I can't hear anything.

SANNE: Now it's stopped. Now it's stopped.

VERNER: I can't see or hear anything.

SANNE: I'm older than she is.

VERNER: It's something else. It's something else.

*BENEDIKTE enters. She's wearing a bathing suit.*

BENEDIKTE: May I join you? –

*SANNE raises herself up.*

SANNE: Sit down.

BENEDIKTE: Have you been in the water? –

SANNE: Not yet.

BENEDIKTE: It looks inviting. It's so blue and inviting and clean.

*JAN enters. He's wearing a bathing suit and has a pair of diver goggles in his hand. For a moment everyone is silent.*

JAN: This is one of the best spots for finding amber. One of the very best. (*To VERNER.*) Want me to show you how? – Come.

*JAN and VERNER walk downstage, in other words down to the water. JAN kneels on one knee. VERNER kneels on one knee next to JAN and together they start looking for amber.*

BENEDIKTE: Did Verner tell you what happened?

SANNE: Yes.

BENEDIKTE: Good.

*JAN and VERNER look for amber.*

(*To SANNE.*) Want to know something strange? – I've never felt so relieved in my life. I know I won't have children. It's my fate. I know that now. It's freed up a lot inside me. I don't know if that's good or bad. But it's set a lot free. I feel like I'd been using all my energy and all my life on longing, and now I've stopped and I feel a great sense of release.

VERNER: I found a piece! I found a piece! –

JAN: Can I see? –

*He takes the piece and bites into it.*

It's amber.

*They stand.*

VERNER: I found a piece of amber! –

*JAN holds the amber up and looks through it at the sun.*

JAN: And there's even a little animal inside. There's a little frozen insect inside it. Isn't that strange? It's stuck inside in exactly the same position it was in millions of years ago. It was sitting on a tree trunk and some sap came rolling down and finally it was trapped and little by little its strength disappeared and since then it's been waiting for us to find it.

*He hands the amber to VERNER.*

*Black.*

# Scene Seven

*The two hotel rooms. Day. The room on the left is empty.*
*BENEDIKTE stands in the room to the right. She has a*
*bathrobe on. She's drying her hair. There's a knock on the*
*door. BENEDIKTE walks over and opens it. JAN enters.*
*He is fully dressed.*

JAN: I just wanted to say I was sorry.

BENEDIKTE: Sorry? –

JAN: For before –

BENEDIKTE: Before? –

JAN: I couldn't have known. How would I have found out?
I mean, you were both so looking forward to it.

*He sits.*

It's strange that all the rooms here are identical. But
they look so different. I mean when there's someone
inside. Isn't that strange? –

BENEDIKTE: I was just getting dressed.

JAN: I never wanted children myself. We never wanted
them. That was the one thing we agreed on. We didn't
want children. I don't understand what they're for. Now
I think I should shut up. You're not the right person to
say this to.

*Silence.*

I'm glad you came again this year. I didn't think you
would. I wasn't expecting to ever see you again. I
thought we'd said goodbye to each other, – we'll never
see them again. And then you came after all. I was so
happy when I heard you two in here. I thought: but
what if it isn't actually them? It could be some strangers.
Maybe they'd be nice. You never know. You never
know if you'll get along. That was why it made me upset

that I said all that. I should have thought before I spoke.
I should have tested the water.

BENEDIKTE: I'm going for a walk with Sanne.

JAN: There's probably more amber on the beach. Would
you like to have some if we find another piece? Would
you? – Maybe we'll find another one with an insect
trapped inside. Those are the finest. The ones with
insects.

*He gets up.*

We've always taken our holiday near the water. But I
actually like the forest more. I've always loved forests.
They close you in. Are you surprised to hear me saying
something like this? That's how I feel inside. They close
in on you. You can lose yourself in them. Or you can
disappear in them. I've always had this thing about
forests. I've never thought they were scary. Even at
night. In the dark. I like the sounds. But also during the
day. When you lie on the forest bed and look up at the
light coming through the branches in long streams. Are
you surprised? –

*Suddenly he grabs at BENEDIKTE, trying to embrace, kiss
and caress her. She fights violently against him. JAN lets
her go, she falls onto the bed, lying there with her face away
from him.*

Sorry. I don't know what I'm doing. Sorry. I just miss
having another person there. Sorry. It's the hurt. I need
someone. I'm sad. Don't cry. You can't cry.

BENEDIKTE: I'm not crying.

*She stands up.*

Okay then.

*She stands in front of JAN.*

Okay then.

*JAN reaches out for her, tries to embrace her, caress her. She stands motionless. JAN stops. Stands a moment completely still with his hands on her. Then suddenly BENEDIKTE answers him, embraces him, squeezes him close, and he embraces her, they are locked together, violent and desperate. They make love.*

*SANNE enters the room on the left. She's still in her bathing suit. A moment later VERNER enters. He is carrying his radio.*

SANNE: I've had too much sun. Would you rub some cream onto my back?

*She hands him something to rub her with. VERNER rubs her with it.*

How did it happen? –

VERNER: How did what happen?

SANNE: With the manager.

VERNER: On the cellar stairs. He was drunk and was going to get another bottle and fell.

SANNE: Who found him? –

VERNER: He crawled up and drove to the doctor. The doctor put his leg in a cast and drove him home.

SANNE: I saw a place where they have raspberries. Should we make something with raspberries? I talked with the manager. He said we could borrow his car. He can't drive it with his broken leg. He can't even get it in the car. Should we borrow his car? Should we take the long way and buy some decent food? Leg of lamb. I love lamb.

VERNER: Or some fish? –

SANNE: I'd rather lamb. With roast potatoes.

VERNER: Roast potatoes? –

SANNE: And then raspberries after.

VERNER: After? –

*In the room to the right they are finished making love.*

After? –

SANNE: What's all this about after? –

VERNER: What about an appetiser? –

SANNE: We can have your fish.

*In the room to the right JAN stands and dresses.*

*BENEDIKTE stays in bed, pulling her bathrobe around her.*

VERNER: Cod roe. I love cod roe. Boiled with lemon.

SANNE: And white wine.

*In the room to the right JAN bends over BENEDIKTE, caressing her face.*

VERNER: Cod roe. Lamb with roast potatoes and raspberry.

*In the room to the right BENEDIKTE's body suddenly begins to cramp up in small tremors. They become more and more violent and suddenly she jumps out of bed, holding her mouth, trying to hold it in. JAN wants to help her but she pushes him away, pushes him toward the door and out, locks the door, leans against it, tries to control the convulsions of her body. Slowly she calms down.*

SANNE: That sounds wonderful.

VERNER: Are you okay now? –

SANNE: Thanks for the help. And thanks for the amber.

VERNER: Amber? –

SANNE: With the insect.

VERNER: Are you going to make earrings? –

SANNE: I doubt it.

VERNER: That's a relief. You want to borrow the radio?
– Everything is easier with music.

SANNE: What for example?

*JAN enters.*

Now we know what we need to do. We'll borrow the
manager's car and drive the long way and get hold of
a leg of lamb. Would you like lamb? I haven't had leg
of lamb in a thousand years. And roast potatoes and
fresh boiled cod roe for an appetiser with lemon and
afterwards raspberries from that place we saw. Doesn't
that sound wonderful? Isn't it enough to make your
mouth water? –

*Black.*

# Scene Eight

*Dining-room. Evening. Candles. Flowers on the table. JAN
and VERNER are sitting at a table. They are a little more
dressed up than usual. There are bottles on the table. The
radio is on the table. On the table there is also a camera.*

VERNER: You know what I mean?

JAN: You want another one? –

VERNER: One more. Let's have one more.

JAN: So we can rest our ears.

*He pours.*

VERNER: As a matter of fact, I've expelled quite a lot of
energy in the name of lust. Believe it or not. Or desire,
rather. I have. And what can I do with that? Can I do
anything with it at all? –

*JAN drinks and pours another. JAN drinks again.*

Of course I have no doubt that it has a place in my
life, but what is that place? Is it simply my life made
manifest? Am I speaking too quickly for you? If I
ignore it, will it become just another lost opportunity
for living life to the full? I sit and eat. Flowers adorn
the table. And there is nothing so banal or obvious as
exposed breasts or bedroom eyes before me. It could be
anything. A nostril. An eyebrow. Haven't you ever been
horny?

JAN: Would you like another? –

*VERNER nods. JAN pours a glass for each of them. JAN
drinks.*

VERNER: Am I boring you? –

JAN: Not at all.

VERNER: Declarations of love for life are always
misunderstood. Better to save our breath.

JAN: Cheers.

*They drink.*

VERNER: Now I know what it was. It was lust. Lust and
love and all those things. What do you say? It's not lust.
It's love. Not love. Not reproduction. Not their worth,
their taste or their dumb habits. Are you with me? It's
gambling with life. Can you tell me why they can't
understand that? Imagine, all this started with the nature
of lust. Where are they, anyway?

JAN: When did Sanne put in the roast? –

VERNER: A half an hour ago.

*He exits the dining-room. JAN pours another glass. Drinks.
VERNER returns.*

The manager says hello and wishes us a pleasant
evening.

JAN: And a pleasant evening to him as well.

VERNER: He's gone to bed with a bottle of whiskey.

*JAN drinks.*

JAN: If you had to lose one of your senses, which one would it be? –

VERNER: Why do you ask? –

JAN: If you had to, which one would it be? –

VERNER: None of them.

JAN: What if you had to? –

VERNER: I won't.

JAN: Sense of smell. I'd lose my sense of smell. And after that, my hearing. And then my sight.

*JAN drinks.*

I've always thought your wife was wonderful. Now don't take that the wrong way. It's just what I've always thought. We're older than the two of you, aren't we? –

VERNER: Older? I've never thought about it.

JAN: You're not offended? –

VERNER: Quite the contrary. I agree.

JAN: Shame about the raspberries.

VERNER: We'll manage without them.

JAN: We'll manage without them.

VERNER: That's what we'll do. Anything left? –

*JAN fills their glasses, they drink. SANNE and BENEDIKTE enter. They're wearing party outfits. BENEDIKTE approaches VERNER.*

BENEDIKTE: Smell me.

*VERNER smells her.*

It's Sanne's.

SANNE: We have the same smell.

*JAN pours drinks for SANNE and BENEDIKTE.*

JAN: Cheers.

*They drink.*

BENEDIKTE: Truth be told, I really didn't want to come back. It was the furthest thing from my mind. But there really isn't anywhere else. Everything was booked, and so we called here as a last resort and of course there was room. I'm glad we came. I'm glad we could spend time with you again. You've both helped me a great deal. I feel like I've finally got over it. Now I know that there's a life for me out there, and that is something that you've given me. You've convinced me that somewhere out there there's life.

*She lifts her glass. They toast.*

Shouldn't we bring a glass to the manager? He's all alone. He can't come here. Shouldn't we go down to him with a glass? Will you come with me Jan? –

*They exit with the bottle.*

SANNE: I went for a walk with Benedikte. Along the beach.

VERNER: What did she say? –

SANNE: The same as she just said.

VERNER: Do you think we'll see each other? –

SANNE: I don't think you'll be able to resist the window-sill with all those tiny pieces of amber.

*JAN and BENEDIKTE return.*

VERNER: Music? Shall we listen to some music? –

SANNE: How is the food doing? –

JAN: The manager said the roast would take an hour and a half.

SANNE: So we have to find some way of entertaining ourselves for an hour and a half.

*VERNER turns on the radio. The volume is unbearably high.*

Turn that down! –

JAN: What?! –

SANNE: Turn it down!!! –

*JAN turns it down.*

JAN: Shall we dance? –

*BENEDIKTE and JAN dance. VERNER dances with SANNE. JAN stops dancing with BENEDIKTE and walks over to SANNE and VERNER. SANNE and JAN dance. BENEDIKTE sings along to the music. VERNER takes out his camera and takes a picture of SANNE and JAN.*

VERNER: I remember the first morning we were here. I couldn't find our room. I went from door to door knocking on all of them. All the rooms looked alike. And all the hallways, too. It's only now that I've begun to find my way around.

*BENEDIKTE starts to dance alone. JAN reaches over to the radio and turns it way up. VERNER turns toward BENEDIKTE and takes a picture of her.*

*Black.*

# YEAR 3

## Scene Nine

*The two hotel rooms. It is early evening. In the room on the left, JAN sits on a chair. He is fully clothed. In the room on the right BENEDIKTE is lying in bed. She raises herself up slightly.*

BENEDIKTE: Verner? Are you there? Verner? – Is that you? Verner is that you?

*She lies down again. SANNE enters the room to the left.*

SANNE: I'm here again. He raised the prices. Isn't that incredible? When you think of how little we actually get for the money. Are you listening to me? Do you want a cigarette? I think he's taking the piss. It's filthy here. And service certainly isn't a word in his vocabulary. Does it bother you? Doesn't it bother you to be paying for something you aren't getting? He stood down there and told me with a straight face – not that he was sober – everything I could possibly want to know about the way that the ocean is slowly but surely eating its way inland all along the coast. They estimated that the hotel would disappear in 2011. How old will we be in 2011? Who says we'll even come back then? In any event the hotel will be gone in 2011 if they don't do anything about it now. Apparently it's quite expensive to put stones out in the water. And that's why he's raised the prices by twenty-five per cent. We ought to think about finding another place. Don't you think? Shouldn't we think about finding some other place? Maybe the only reason we keep coming back is the fact that we don't know any other place to go. Who knows, there might be some wonderful place just a kilometre from here. Maybe not even a kilometre. A little further inland so they don't start raising their rates. We ought to go look around. We've never seen anything here except the

44

hotel. We should go to the museum. Would you like that? Would you like to go to the museum? Would you? We've talked about it so many times. Who knows what kind of little treasures they've got hidden there? –

*She walks over to JAN, bends down so that her face is near his, as though she was going to kiss him.*

I thought there was a crumb there.

*She removes it.*

All better. The manager said the others had arrived. I haven't heard any noises from their room. Did you hear them while I was out? Did you? –

*JAN shakes his head.*

I don't want to say hello to them just yet. I don't want to disturb them. Tomorrow. Tomorrow we can all go down to the beach together. Would you like that? Would you like to go down to the beach a get a little sun? –

Who knows, maybe you'll feel like having a little look down by the water, maybe you'll find some pretty pieces of amber? –

*JAN tries to say something, but it comes out as a completely incomprehensible, rattling sound.*

Are you trying to say something? –

*JAN tries again.*

Try saying it more slowly.

*JAN tries again.*

For the life of me, I can't understand you. Remember what she told you to do. Take deep breaths. Relax. Sit up straight.

*She adjusts his pillow.*

Now try again. –

JAN: I…

SANNE: I? –

*JAN nods, relieved.*

I what? –

*JAN again produces the rattling sound.*

When? Whip? Wound? –

*JAN shakes his head vehemently.*

I'm trying my best to help you. But I need you to help, too. You have to do something. You have to help. What are you trying to say? –

*JAN again emits a sound.*

Chair? Care? –

*JAN nods energetically.*

You care? –

JAN: (*With great difficulty.*) Don't –

SANNE: You don't care about what? –

JAN: Ag…

SANNE: Brag? –

*JAN shakes his head.*

JAN: B…

SANNE: Be. You don't want to be what? –

*JAN makes a sound.*

I don't understand. I can't understand you. Try again from the beginning. You don't want what? –

*JAN fights to make a sound.*

Poor thing. You mustn't let this get to you. I'm here to help you. We'll pull through this, she's promised that everything will be alright again. If you do your exercises, everything will be better again. That's what she promised.

*JAN shakes his head. Finally JAN struggles the right word out, with violent, intense energy.*

JAN: Together! Together! –

*JAN collapses back into his chair, exhausted. SANNE bends over him, clumsily embracing him.*

SANNE: Why don't you want to be together? –

*She walks away from him.*

Why don't you want to be together?

*In the room to the right, BENEDIKTE sits up in bed.*

BENEDIKTE: Verner? –

*A moment later VERNER enters the room. He is carrying the radio and a suitcase.*

I knew you would come just now. I couldn't hear you, but I knew it anyway. I knew you would come. You've been down to get the luggage. But you didn't come right up. You went down and saw the suitcase and the radio out there on the stairs and suddenly you felt like walking down to the water. You felt like walking down to the water even though it's cold and getting dark. You walked down to the water. You walked down and stood there by the water. You looked out over it. You stood out there in the surf and you didn't care that it made your shoes all wet. Your shoes are wet now. True? You have wet shoes. I've been watching the sky. It's grey and dark blue and the sun is hidden behind the clouds. The sun is orange and white and purple. True? You were disappointed you didn't have your camera with you. You would have liked to take a picture. Then you thought of me. I could feel it. You thought of me and came back and brought up the suitcase and the radio.

Am I right? Wasn't that what you did? Didn't I feel it? Didn't I? Didn't I?? –

*Black.*

# Scene Ten

*The beach. SANNE is sunbathing. A few metres away from her sits JAN, wrapped up in blankets. VERNER stands. The radio is somewhere nearby.*

VERNER: What happened? –

SANNE: Happened? –

VERNER: What happened? –

SANNE: Did something happen? –

VERNER: Why didn't you call? –

*VERNER turns on the radio.*

I so enjoyed our meetings.

*Music.*

What happened to Jan? –

SANNE: He killed himself. Or he tried to. I told him that I wanted out. I decided after we came home last summer. So he took a bottle of whisky and a bottle of sleeping pills and lay down in the forest behind the house. It wasn't that original, but it went wrong anyway. I think the plan was that I was supposed to have found him earlier. But there was a traffic jam and I got home twenty minutes later than usual. He left a letter where he tried to say all the things he couldn't say while he was alive. In any event, he tried. So I went out and found him. He'd been without oxygen for too long, and now he can't talk.

VERNER: Why did you want out? –

SANNE: To be alone.

*VERNER looks at JAN.*

He's sleeping. He's taken something to relax.

VERNER: Why didn't you call? –

SANNE: I couldn't do that to Jan.

VERNER: Did you want to? –

SANNE: I didn't want to touch you with a ten-foot pole.

VERNER: I thought we had an agreement. I thought we were going to see each other more often.

SANNE: That was before.

VERNER: Why wouldn't you touch me with a ten foot pole? –

SANNE: I didn't feel like it. I've been with so many. I just didn't want more. I've never been with someone that couldn't talk. It's something new. Benedikte is waving.

*SANNE waves over the audience. VERNER waves as well.*

What have you been up to? –

VERNER: One day I came home and the fridge was completely empty. 'I can't stand the sight of food,' she tells me. 'What about eating?' I asked. 'When I get hungry again I will eat what my body tells me to eat.' She's started to listen to her body again. That's what she says. 'I've started listening to my body.'

SANNE: Jan will soon be able to move normally again. All that's left is the speaking. They say he'll be able to. He'll speak again. There may be a few consonants that give him trouble. But that's all. He'll be himself again.

VERNER: Everything between us has slowed to a halt.

SANNE: Is that a change? –

VERNER: From nothing to nothing at all.

*They laugh.*

You are the only person I can talk to. I can't talk to her. I never could talk to her. I don't know why it's easier to talk to you. I mean, of course we can talk. But it doesn't mean anything for me. It doesn't touch me. I slide off it. That's what I do. I slide off it. Off her. I slide off it.

SANNE: You remind me of someone.

VERNER: Do I? Who? –

SANNE: You.

*Silence.*

She's waving again.

*SANNE waves to BENEDIKTE.*

Wave to her.

*VERNER waves.*

It must be tough for you.

VERNER: Don't feel sorry for me. I have my own road to follow.

*JAN stirs. VERNER stands and walks over to him.*

I got a promotion. I'm still at the same company and I got a promotion. Now you have to run even faster to keep the treadmill going. I had the pictures from last year developed. Some of them came out well. Especially the ones of you dancing. You and Sanne dancing. You're wrapped in each other's arms and dancing. You can just see Benedikte in the background. You're smiling at me. That was the best picture of the bunch.

*Black.*

# Scene Eleven

*The two hotel rooms. Day. In the room to the left is SANNE. In the room to the right is BENEDIKTE. She is putting on make-up. When she finishes, she stands. She leaves the room.*

*There is a knock on the door in the room to the left. SANNE opens the door.*

SANNE: Come in.

*BENEDIKTE enters.*

BENEDIKTE: Why did you wave? –

SANNE: Because you did.

BENEDIKTE: Was that why you waved? –

SANNE: I waved to wave back.

BENEDIKTE: I was diving. I dove down and disappeared. If you looked out over the water you would have seen me. Were you looking? –

SANNE: I saw you wave.

BENEDIKTE: Sound is far away underwater. I tried to hit two stones together. 'Clunk, clunk,' they said. Far, far away.

SANNE: But it wasn't for me.

BENEDIKTE: Was that why you waved? –

SANNE: Because of the clunk, clunk? I obviously couldn't hear that. I couldn't hear that because you were deep down under the water and all the sounds were far away.

*Silence.*

BENEDIKTE: Why isn't Jan speaking? –

SANNE: There isn't much to say. What would speaking help? I could also say all kinds of things to you. And I imagine you could as well. But what would it help? –

BENEDIKTE: Why did he stop talking? –

SANNE: Some people never stop, others do. We're all different. Is there something you would like to say to me? –

BENEDIKTE: I could never ever just throw myself down on a beach. Do you know how many little animals there are there? If you sift through the sand with your fingers you find thousands. You crush them. You can't just throw yourself on them. You can't. All the little animals would be crushed.

SANNE: Not on a beach. Not on a beach. The sand evens out the weight. You don't crush anything. Nature is cleverly put together. Not even the big animals. You don't even crush the big animals.

BENEDIKTE: Scary animals? –

SANNE: No, big animals. Lizards or crabs. For example.

BENEDIKTE: Scary animals –

SANNE: Are you somehow quite mad?

*BENEDIKTE sits.*

BENEDIKTE: Do you have children? –

SANNE: Do you see any? –

BENEDIKTE: Do you want to? –

SANNE: When I one day vanish from the face of the earth, I want no sign of me left behind. There will be no sorrow or pain. Or as little as possible. I hope to slip away into a tiny, anonymous, dark place without tears.

BENEDIKTE: I know about you. You and Verner.

SANNE: What do you know? –

BENEDIKTE: You long to hear someone tell you they love you.

SANNE: Shall we find the others? –

BENEDIKTE: There's no need. They've gone for a walk. What else would they do? They've gone for a walk along the water and every now and then Verner looks up here and wonders what we're doing. He doesn't know where we are. He doesn't know. And he never will.

*BENEDIKTE cautiously begins to sing.*

Have you ever heard me sing before? –

SANNE: I think I heard you down on the beach once.

BENEDIKTE: Were you with Verner? –

SANNE: I believe so.

BENEDIKTE: I know you heard me. I was lying down, looking at you. I was hiding up on the cliff. I lay there and watched you. I couldn't hear you. I could only see what you were saying.

*BENEDIKTE sings softly again.*

Afterwards I came down to you. I sat next to you. Do you remember? I sat next to you and told you about my release. I told you about my relief. I said that I'd been set free. Do you remember that? There is nothing that ties me down any more. Nothing. I am as free as a bird. I can fly away if I want to.

*Silence.*

Will you hold me? Will you? Will you hold me? –

SANNE: I think I can hear them.

*BENEDIKTE stands and walks over to SANNE.*

BENEDIKTE: Will you? Will you hold me? –

*SANNE remains standing. BENEDIKTE leans up against her. She stands with her arms relaxed. SANNE embraces her clumsily.*

It's good to be embraced.

SANNE: Benedikte? Will you listen to me? Benedikte? You're going to have to take care of yourself. Will you? –

*Black.*

\* \* \*

*The two hotel rooms. Night. In the room to the left SANNE is helping JAN out of his clothes. In the room to the right VERNER is taking off his clothes. BENEDIKTE is sitting on the bed.*

BENEDIKTE: Tell me something.

VERNER: What? –

BENEDIKTE: Anything.

VERNER: I don't know what to tell you.

BENEDIKTE: Tell me about the walk on the beach.

VERNER: We walked along the beach. We saw lots of water and lots of sand. It was a little windy. Otherwise not much else happened.

BENEDIKTE: Did you talk? –

VERNER: I talked a little. Jan didn't say much. Or rather, I didn't have the patience to let him say too much. I told him about my job. I don't know if he was interested. That was all.

BENEDIKTE: Would you ever leave me? –

VERNER: Never. Would you? –

BENEDIKTE: What? –

VERNER: Leave me? –

BENEDIKTE: Never. I'm afraid.

VERNER: That I'm going to leave you? Don't be. I won't.

BENEDIKTE: That's not what I'm afraid of.

VERNER: What then? –

BENEDIKTE: I don't know.

VERNER: You have to be afraid of something! What are you afraid of?! –

BENEDIKTE: I don't know.

VERNER: You're just afraid? –

BENEDIKTE: Can you hear me singing? –

*BENEDIKTE sings cautiously, softly. VERNER shakes her violently. Then he stands still, looking at her.*

*Black.*

## Scene Twelve

*Dining-room. Outside the sun is going down. BENEDIKTE and JAN sit with their back to the window. JAN has pillows and blankets arranged around him. He watches the sunset. SANNE and VERNER sit a little way off. SANNE is wearing amber earrings. There is a bottle on the table.*

VERNER: You had earrings made? –

SANNE: How did you know? – Jan found two pieces of amber last year. One of them has an insect in it. See! – I love these earrings. They remind me of good times. I can still see him now crawling around looking for amber for me. Now I'm happy he did.

VERNER: Did you see he raised the prices by twenty-five per cent?

SANNE: I know.

VERNER: He told this long sob story about the coastline moving in. Something about how if they don't do anything now the hotel would be gone by 2011.

SANNE: I know.

VERNER: They want to put rocks out on the beach. I didn't really understand what he meant by that. He wasn't sober. I actually couldn't understand what he was saying. But it was something about rocks. It was something about rocks splitting the stream in the water. Or breaking it. I think that's what he said. They want to put rocks out to break the stream and stop the water from eating away at the beach.

SANNE: I know.

VERNER: Twenty-five per cent is a steep increase. You have to ask yourself whether it's worth it. The service is already pretty bad. Isn't that right? It doesn't exactly make you jump for joy.

BENEDIKTE: I think it's good. And I think it's evil.

*BENEDIKTE doesn't turn to face the others.*

VERNER: I don't want any more.

BENEDIKTE: That's what I think. I think there are good and evil things. Good and evil. I think that the path between them goes through the body. We've been given these bodies. We've been put inside them. But evil is in this world and when evil is in this world then it is also in these bodies.

VERNER: Will you help me stop her? –

*SANNE remains sitting.*

BENEDIKTE: You can work against your body and that's evil work. That's what evil means for me. You can listen to your body. You can learn to listen to your body. Hear its whisper and call and little signals. You can learn to speak with it. And if you listen to it and do what it tells you then you are good. I have been bad at listening. I've turned a deaf ear to its call. I've only just begun to listen. Maybe I had to go through all these things in order to begin listening. But maybe it's already too late. I have the evil in me.

*VERNER stands while she speaks and walks over to her.*

VERNER: I think you should go upstairs now. Shall we? –

BENEDIKTE: I'm not going up.

VERNER: Aren't you tired? –

BENEDIKTE: I can sleep later.

*JAN tries to find the right words.*

SANNE: Would you like some more to drink? Is that what you're trying to say? More to drink? –

*JAN shakes his head. SANNE pours him more to drink.*

BENEDIKTE: My fingers are like matches. Tiny, thin matches. When I move them they make snapping sounds.

SANNE: They won't break.

VERNER: I think we're going upstairs now. I think we're going to go up and have a rest.

*BENEDIKTE speaks directly to SANNE now, very intensely:*

BENEDIKTE: It doesn't matter if they hear us. It doesn't matter. It's fine if they do. I'm trying to explain it to you. I have the evil in me. Do you understand what I'm saying? I have the evil in me.

*SANNE starts to laugh hysterically. She grabs BENEDIKTE and dances with her. VERNER pulls BENEDIKTE away from her.*

VERNER: (*Tenderly.*) Come Benedikte.

BENEDIKTE: I want you to stay down here. Won't you please? I'd rather go upstairs alone.

*She starts to leave. JAN stands. He blocks her way. For a moment everything is frozen. He tries to say something but can't. He gives up and reaches for her, grabs her face, squeezing it between his hands. For a moment everything is quiet. SANNE walks over to him and carefully pulls him away from BENEDIKTE. BENEDIKTE waves to him. She exits. JAN collapses in tears. SANNE goes to him, puts her arm around him and leads him to a chair. Gives him something to drink.*

VERNER: And that's how their last night together ended that year.

*Black.*

# YEAR 4

## Scene Thirteen

*The two hotel rooms. Night. In the room to the right sits VERNER. The light is low. The radio is on the table. It plays music, soft music. VERNER is sitting very still.*

*In the room to the left is a bottle of champagne in a cooler in the middle of the floor. The light is on. JAN stands by the window. He is practising speaking. Each letter he says is slightly different:*

JAN: S. S. S. T. T. T. D. D. D.

*SANNE is walking around the room lighting candles. She has the earrings on.*

Would you like me to bring him here? –

*JAN turns off the light and leaves the room.*

*A moment later there's a knock on the door in the room to the right. VERNER doesn't react. JAN cautiously opens the door. VERNER slowly stands and leaves with JAN. The radio continues to play after they leave.*

*VERNER and JAN enter the room to the left. SANNE walks over to VERNER and embraces him.*

SANNE: Good to see you again. Won't you sit down? –

*VERNER sits on the bed. JAN pours drinks for everyone.*

I think it's nicer to be up here. It isn't very cosy downstairs.

JAN: The bottle is compliments of the manager. He claims it's our tenth year here. I think it's only nine. But I'll hold my tongue for a bottle of champagne. Cheers! –

SANNE: Cheers! –

*They drink.*

The manager looks like a crazy man with those glasses.

JAN: He's got new glasses? –

SANNE: Didn't you notice? Like big, thick magnifying glasses. He must have been nearly blind all these years. Bad eyesight isn't something that you just get from one day to the next.

JAN: My goodness, that means he was just blind all those times we thought he was drunk. You learn something new every day. Or maybe now he's both drunk and blind. Cheers! –

SANNE: Cheers Verner! –

*They drink.*

JAN: That reminds me, I found a bunch of pictures. Over twenty, I think. All of them of you, Verner. In your room.

SANNE: Cheers! –

*JAN looks for the pictures.*

Jan has been quite good about practising his speech. He does exercises every morning. Who else would have the strength to learn to speak at his age?

*JAN finds the pictures.*

JAN: Now take a look at these. They're all of you. A whole roll. Only you. Picture after picture. Only you.

*JAN shows him the pictures.*

We must have been drunk. Otherwise I have no idea why I would take so many of you. I made copies. These are for you. A gift for you.

SANNE: Can I take a look? –

JAN: You've seen them.

SANNE: I'd like to see them again.

*JAN hands her the pictures.*

You haven't changed a bit.

JAN: I remembered my camera this time.

*He shows them his camera.*

Sit over there next to him. –

SANNE: No pictures. Not now.

JAN: Oh come on.

*SANNE sits next to VERNER.*

Put your arm around Verner's shoulders.

*She does.*

Look over here! –

*JAN takes a picture.*

Try looking a little happier! –

*JAN takes another picture.*

SANNE: Shhh! –

JAN: What is it? –

SANNE: The music. Can't you hear the music? Someone's singing.

*Black.*

# Scene Fourteen

*Dining-room. Day. SANNE and JAN are seated, eating breakfast. SANE has her amber earrings on.*

JAN: I couldn't sleep.

SANNE: I was awake most of the night. You didn't wake up as far as I could tell.

JAN: I slept an hour. Then I woke up and couldn't fall asleep again.

SANNE: Either you were very quiet or you slept more than you think.

*VERNER enters. He has a little box in his hand. He sits down at another table. SANNE stands.*

Would you like me to get something for you? What would you like? Coffee? Juice? A roll? Cheese and marmalade? – Coffee, juice, rolls, cheese and marmalade.

*VERNER doesn't answer. SANNE remains standing.*

JAN: It's windy outside. I think it will rain. Maybe it will get warmer. Maybe we'll be able to dive and sunbathe. It's too cold to go in the water now.

SANNE: Maybe it will get warmer.

JAN: Would you like to go lie on the beach? –

SANNE: I'd like to get some sun on this body.

*VERNER stands and walks to their table. He brings the box. He places it on the table, opens it and pushes it over to SANNE and JAN.*

VERNER: Want to see? –

SANNE: What is it? –

JAN: Pictures.

*He takes the pictures out of the box and looks at them.*

SANNE: What are they of? –

JAN: (*To VERNER.*) I can't make them out –

*He gives them to SANNE.*

SANNE: Toes. It's toes. They're toes! –

VERNER: I didn't have my camera with me. I was allowed to go home and get it and come back. I love those toes. There is a softness in them, isn't there? Those tiny toes. Look at them. Especially the nails on the little toes. Aren't they sweet? They're so small they almost aren't there. They're almost gone. That's what makes them so sweet. They're happy toes. Happy toes. They could be a little baby's. You get the urge to hold them. To hold them in your hand. Isn't that right? Aren't they the most beautiful toes you've ever seen? – They're so beautiful you almost can't stand it.

*VERNER gathers up the pictures, puts them back in the box.*

Are you coming again next year? –

SANNE: I think so. Are you? –

VERNER: I'm coming. I'll come again. Where else would I go? –

*Black.*

## Scene Fifteen

*The beach. Blinding light of day. It's windy and cold. JAN and SANNE come walking. They have big coats on. She's wearing her amber earrings.*

SANNE: I asked him if he wanted coffee or a roll or juice. Cheese and marmalade. But he didn't want anything. I really tried to do something for him.

*JAN waves. SANNE waves as well. They wave away from the audience, with their backs toward them.*

Who are we waving to? –

JAN: The manager. He's just come out.

*They stop waving, turn toward the audience. Look out over the ocean.*

Would you like to eat lunch with Verner and get a little tipsy? Isn't tipsy just what we need right now. Isn't it? Isn't it just what we need? A little tipsy.

SANNE: Jan? –

JAN: S. S. S. D. D. D. T. T. T.

*He is walking away from her.*

SANNE: If I die first... If you are left behind... Will you say beautiful things about me? Will you say beautiful things about me? Will you? If I die first? –

JAN: O. O. O. A. A. A.

*Black.*

www.ingramcontent.com/pod-product-compliance
Ingram Content Group UK Ltd.
Pitfield, Milton Keynes, MK11 3LW, UK
UKHW020729280225
455688UK00012B/561